# Famous Landmarks

by Mary Clare Goller

# I need to know these words.

bridge

buildings

landmark

**lighthouse**

**mountain**

**statue**

Do you send postcards?
A postcard can show a bridge.
A bridge can be a landmark.

▲ The Brooklyn Bridge lets people cross the river.

This bridge is a landmark.
Many people cross this bridge.
This bridge is a busy highway.

New York, NY

▲ This bridge connects two parts of New York City.

Many people visit the United States.
People come from different lands.

San Francisco, CA

▲ The Golden Gate Bridge is in San Francisco.

People visit this bridge.
This bridge is a landmark.

▲ Many people visit the
Golden Gate Bridge.

Some buildings are landmarks. This landmark reminds some people of outer space.

Seattle, WA

▲ This building is called the Space Needle.

You can visit the top of this landmark. You can see the whole city.

◄ The Space Needle is in Seattle, Washington.

This lighthouse guides sailors to shore. The sailors can see the light from many miles away.

Cape Hatteras, NC

▲ The Cape Hatteras lighthouse is in North Carolina.

People built the lighthouse long ago. The lighthouse still stands!

▲ This lighthouse is the tallest lighthouse in the United States.

This mountain is a landmark.
You can see four faces in
this mountain.

Keystone, SD

▲ The four faces in Mount Rushmore
show presidents of the United States.

Many workers carved the faces.
The work lasted fourteen years.

▲ The Native American leader Crazy Horse is honored near Mount Rushmore.

# Do you know this landmark?
# The statue is a symbol of freedom.

New York, NY

▲ The Statue of Liberty welcomes people to the United States.

Another name for this statue
is Lady Liberty.

◄ This arm is more
than forty feet long.

Can you match the cities on this map to their landmarks? What landmark is near you?

Seattle, WA

Keystone, SD

New York, NY

San Francisco, CA

Cape Hatteras, NC